The Ten Things You Must Do
Before You Retire
By
Ken Mahoney

ISBN 978-0-9980047-2-3

The mission of Mahoney Asset Management
Know our clients well
Anticipate their needs
Exceed their expectations!

Contents

About the Author – Ken Mahoney

Licensed financial advisor for 31 years, investor, and author of 9 books including The Ten Things You Must Do Before You Retire, Ken Mahoney is the CEO of Mahoney Asset Management.

Because of Ken's comprehensive financial expertise, he is a regular guest contributor on the Fox Business programs "Mornings with

Maria" hosted by Maria Bartiromo and "Making Money with Charles Payne" hosted by Charles Payne. In addition, Ken has appeared on The Today Show, CBS, ABC and WPIX. He has been quoted in numerous national

publications such as *USA Today, Associated Press, U.S. News and World Report* and *The Wall Street Journal*. Ken also provides daily market updates on several radio stations including WRCR AM 1700, WHUD FM 100.7 and WXPK FM 107.1 *The Peak* and publishes a weekly newsletter *The Smart Investor*. Ken was recruited to serve on the House of Representatives Banking and Services. In this capacity, he advised the Chairperson of the Committee, Sue Kelly, on the impact of new financial regulations, Federal Reserve Bank transparency, and guided the Committee in asking questions of Alan Greenspan.

A believer in giving back, Ken has been serving his community for more than two decades volunteering as a member of Meals On Wheels and The United Way. Currently serving as chairman of the alumni board at Make-A-Wish Foundation, Ken led the most successful fundraising campaign at the time as former Chairman of the Board. Acknowledged by the New York State Legislature for his dedication and outstanding community service, Ken was honored with a Distinguished Service Award and chosen by Rockland County as community leader of the year.

Ken has 3 sons, Brendan, Connor and Kenny. Ken is married to Kelly C Dantas. Ken enjoys reading, sports and music. His favorite author is Dr Wayne Dyer, and he still listens to classic rock!

Preface

What makes this book different is that it is action oriented to help you get organized and take control. At the end of each chapter you will find a checklist of action items you must do to prepare for retirement and at the end of the book you check off what you did, and you can see what is deficient. Successful retirement's do not happen by chance. Like any other long-term endeavor, it requires planning, forethought, and consideration of all possible scenarios and their consequences.

This book is different than the other books I have written, because it's meant to be an 'action guide'. The concepts that we cover in this book need to be addressed in order to have a fully engaged and purposeful retirement.

You may have heard that you have to wait until you are 65, 70, or even older to be financially independent, retired, and living life the way you want to be living it and doing what you want to do.

As you go through the chapters, you may realize that you have already completed some of ten things you need to do. That's great. I would then ask you to look at the other chapters where you need to 'check the box', and complete.

I want to thank Megan Kennedy for her hard work in editing this book. Without Megan, this book would not exist!

Chapter 1: Know Where You Are Now

A successful retirement will require planning. Knowing where you are now is the first important step and requires taking an in-depth inventory of what you have.

If you've ever been driving in unknown territory then you are likely familiar with turning on your GPS device, plugging in the address of your destination, and following the directions to get where you want to go.

In order to provide you with the best route it is essential that you enter your current location because if you don't, you could end up going way off course. Even with the best GPS device, not having a proper starting point, won't allow it to provide you with the best route.

It's also important to have the most updated GPS application. That's because there may be new roads to take, or alternatively, roads that are either under construction or no longer available. Planning for retirement can be a similar process.

The Changing Nature of Retirement

When it comes to planning your best route to retirement, you will need to have a good idea of what you want to do when you get there. While many people dream about how it will be when they can control their time, having a successful retirement will require that you have a purpose and that you are emotionally prepared.

If you've worked for most of your life, you may see yourself as being "what you do" - many people, whether intentional or not, define themselves by their career.

Starting on the day that you retire that will all change. Therefore, it is essential to have goals, activities and an overall sense of purpose even after you leave your employer. Doing so can make each and every day in retirement more rewarding.

You will also need to know what is and isn't an option for you. What used to provide the retirees of yesterday with the income that was needed may not be open to you today. In fact, the way in which we retire has changed considerably over time. In the past, retirees typically had three key income sources. These included a defined benefit pension, Social Security, and personal savings and investments.

Disappearing Pension Income

In just a generation, the nature of retirement and retirement planning has significantly changed. Gone are the days of working for just one employer, receiving a gold watch after twenty-five years of service and being assured that pension income will last throughout one's "golden years". Today, we are living and working longer than previous generations, we change jobs and/or careers far more often and we are now responsible for our own savings.

Yesterday, the idea of saving for one's retirement outside of the work environment was rare. Most companies provided a defined pension plan for employees. These types of plans pay out a specific amount of money, based on salary history and years of service, to retired employees, with those payouts guaranteed for the rest of their life. Organizations whose employees are part of a union (e.g., teachers, police and fire departments) are among the few who are currently fortunate enough to enjoy the benefit of a defined pension plan.

Today, few companies provide a defined benefit plan. Instead, in part because of the associated high costs and complex nature of the plans, companies have essentially placed the responsibility solely on the employees to make contributions (e.g., payroll deductions) to defined contribution plans like 401(k) and 403(b) plans.

Uncertain Social Security

Social Security may be a source of income during retirement, but according to the Social Security Administration, "Social Security was never meant to be the only source of income for people when they retire. Social Security replaces about 40 percent of an average wage earner's income after retiring."

In addition, the Social Security Administration notes "As a result of changes to Social Security enacted in 1983, benefits are now expected to be payable in full on a timely basis until 2037, when the trust fund reserves are projected to become exhausted. At the point where the reserves are used up, continuing taxes are expected to be enough to pay 76 percent of scheduled benefits". [1]

It is unlikely social security will provide you with enough income to support the lifestyle you hope for in retirement.

Personal Savings and Investments

Another source of retirement income includes personal savings and investments. While many retirees in the past did not need to rely solely on this source of income generation, today it is much more important. This is especially true given the disappearance of defined benefit pension plans as well as the uncertainty that surrounds Social Security.

Get Organized

The first step to knowing where you are now is to get organized. Make a list of all financial accounts including checking, savings, non-retirement investment and retirement investment. Be sure to account for retirement accounts (e.g., 401(k), 403(b)) you may have from previous employers. As you are creating the list, collect the most recent statement for each account. Doing so may entail contacting, by phone or internet, financial institutions for current copies. Next, set up a filing system using folders or a binder with tabs to identify each account.

Once you have accounted for and organized your accounts, review the title or registration of each account to ensure they are current. You want to be sure the name(s) associated with the account(s) is correct. For example, do you still own a jointly held account with an ex-spouse or another person who may have passed away? If so, contact the financial institution to determine how to update the title.

At the same time review the status of any designated beneficiaries. As life events take place like divorce or death beneficiary designations need to be updated. Keep in mind beneficiary designations are not limited to retirement accounts (e.g., IRAs, 401(k)s). Did you establish a "TOD" or "transfer on death" non-retirement account, which allows for the account assets to transfer directly to designated beneficiary upon your death and is the beneficiary designation current? You will need to contact the financial institution where the account is held to determine what is needed, if necessary, to update the designation.

And while you are organizing, some general record retention timeframes are as follows:

- Tax records including tax returns, tax payments, tax related correspondence and notices – at least seven years
- Property records relating to deeds, mortgages and leases – until disposition of property plus six years
- Birth and death certificates - forever
- Life insurance policies – until policy ends
- Medical records - forever
- Financial statements – one to three years
- Vehicle records – until sold
- Sales receipts- for the length of the warranty period
- Credit card statements – one to three years
- Savings accounts
- Investments accounts
- Retirement accounts (IRAs, 401(k)s)
- Personal Residence
- Rental Property
- Vacation Home
- Collectibles (art, coins, stamps, etc.)
- Jewelry
- Automobile
- Social Security

What You Own and What You Owe

In order to determine where you currently stand in terms of your finances and to come up with your "starting point" it is important to come up with good, solid figures on how much you own and how much you owe.

The best way to do this is to create a detailed list of your assets and liabilities.

Assets

Assets are defined as items that have economic value and are expected to provide future benefit and include the following:

- Savings accounts
- Investments accounts
- Retirement accounts (IRAs, 401(k)s)
- Personal Residence
- Rental Property
- Vacation Home
- Collectibles (art, coins, stamps, etc.)
- Jewelry
- Automobile
- Social Security

Liabilities

While assets are things that you own, liabilities are what you owe, otherwise referred to as debt obligations. Some examples of liabilities include:

- Home mortgage
- Home equity loan
- Auto loan(s)
- Personal loan(s)
- Credit card balance(s)

Add up the total amount of your assets and subtract the amount of your total liabilities to calculate your overall net worth.

Take Advantage of Saving and Investment Opportunities – Employer Sponsored Plans

By taking advantage of saving and investment opportunities you can increase the amount of your assets and, provided that you keep the amount of your liabilities in check, you can also increase the amount of your total net worth.

One of the best ways you can increase the amount in your asset column is to participate in your employer's retirement plan. The most common plan offered by a privately held or publicly held company is a 401(k), while government entities, non-profits and school districts offer a 403(b). There can be a number of advantages to participating.

Tax Deferral

When you make a contribution to most retirement plans, you can reduce the amount of taxable income by the amount contributed to the plan.

Contributions to a 401(k) are deducted from wages so the amount of wages reported to the IRS by an employer is reduced by the amount of the contributions.

In addition, as a result of the reduced amount of wages reported to the IRS, the amount of wages subject to withholding is reduced.

The following chart shows the future value and investment return differences between tax and tax-deferred:

Age	30	40	50
Initial Investment	$50,000	$50,000	$50,000
Expected Annual Rate of Return	6%	6%	6%
Number of Years Invested	35	25	15
Distribution Age	65	65	65
Marginal Tax Rate	22%	22%	22%
Investment Return Taxable	6%	6%	6%
Taxable Account Value	$247,856	$156,878	$99,294
Tax Deferred Account Value	$374,381	$210,620	$118,491

https://financialmentor.com/calculator/taxable-vs-tax-deferred-calculator

Matching

Many companies will "match" a percentage of the employee's contribution which is often referred to as "free money." A matching contribution provides additional funds in your account over and above your personal deferrals. Even if your employer does not offer a matching contribution you are only doing yourself a disservice by not contributing even a small amount from your wages.

Diversity

401(k) plans provide a variety of different investment options to choose from. These may include:

- Money Market Funds
- Stock and bond mutual funds
- Employer company stock

All plans offer investments with varying degrees of risk and reward so employees can choose which option or options will work the best for them depending on specific goals

Compound Interest

Albert Einstein is to have said "Compound interest is the eighth wonder of the world. He who understands it, earns it; he who doesn't, pays it." Compound interest is the method of calculating interest whereby interest earned over time is added to the principal – simply put 'interest on interest'.

A simple compound interest calculator shows the future value of an initial $5,000.00 investment:

Initial investment:	$5,000.00
Additional investment annually:	$1,000.00
Years to grow:	10
Interest rate:	5%
Future value:	$21,351.26

Compounded one time annually

Assessing Your Retirement Ability

In planning for retirement and determining where you are now, it is essential to get a "snapshot" of your finances. However, there are other factors that are also important in helping you to prepare for this time in your life. This is because other criteria will have an impact on how much retirement income you may require.

Health Factors

In addition to determining your assets and liabilities, another important factor to consider is the status of your health. Are you currently in good health?

A recent analysis by Fidelity Investments estimated that a 65-year-old couple retiring in 2019 will need an estimated $285,000 to cover health care costs in retirement.

While Medicare will help to cover some of the costs, those enrolled in Medicare will still have a number of out-of-pocket co-payments and deductibles that they are responsible for paying.

The $285,000 in health care costs does not take into account the possibility of needing long-term care and it is estimated that 7 in 10 retirees who are over age 65 will need at least some form of long-term care services in their lifetime.[3] Long-term care can be extremely expensive. According to Genworth's 2018 Cost of Care Survey, the national median monthly rate for a private room in a skilled nursing facility was $8,365.[4] This equates to over $100,000 per year.

Even the need for home health care for basic assistance with everyday activities such as bathing, and dressing can be quite costly. On average, the national median weekly rate for home health aide and homemaker services was $4,195 per week in 2018.[5] Unfortunately, Medicare pays very little for skilled nursing facility care and even less for home health care services.

If you do qualify for Medicare's skilled nursing home benefit you could still be responsible for paying a substantial amount in terms of co-insurance. Currently, Medicare will pay the tab for the first 20 days of your stay, however, after day 20 co-insurance charges would apply.[6]

Because of the need for health care in retirement, combined with the escalating costs, it is necessary to include these costs in your planning.

Social Security

While there is uncertainty and concern with the long-term viability of Social Security it is a current source of income and you should review the status of your benefits. The Social Security Administration issues statements once every five years from age 25 to 60 and then yearly until you start receiving benefits. To determine your current estimated benefit, visit the Social Security website (www.socialsecurity.gov/estimator) to use the Retirement Estimator. To review your statement, visit the My Account section of the website (www.socialsecurity.gov/myaccount).

You can begin to apply for and receive Social Security benefits at age 62 but delaying until age 70 will result in a larger benefit - it could increase by as much as 8 percent. Per the Social Security Administration, if you were born after 1960 your full retirement age is 67.

The average monthly Social Security benefit in 2019 is $1,461. The maximum payout for someone who files at full retirement age, currently 66, is $2,861 and $3,770 for someone who files at age 70. You would need to earn the maximum taxable amount of $132,900 over a 35-year career to receive the monthly benefit of $2,861.

If you plan on working in retirement and collecting social security before you reach your full retirement age, you must bear in mind that if you earn more than $17,640 (the limit for 2019), Social Security deducts $1 from your benefits for every $2 you earn.

Desire, Need and Ability to Work

Even though many people may consider retirement as a time to stop working, having a paid position may be something you will need or want to do down the road. For some, starting a new business or taking on a job in a different field is something that is anticipated.

For others, however, due to the need for additional income to cover living expenses, working in retirement may be a necessity. If this is you, it will be important to get an approximate calculation of how much you will need for your living expenses in retirement and then determine how much you will have coming in from various sources. If you find there is a "gap," now is the time to make a plan for filling in the additional income you will need.

Are You Prepared to Move Forward?

Are you prepared to do what is necessary in order to achieve retirement security? Moving forward requires knowing what you have and setting clear cut goals - both financially and emotionally - and then doing what it takes in order to accomplish them.

Getting to your milestone requires that you get into the proper mindset as you move forward. In doing so you will then be better prepared to take the financial actions that you need in order to achieve your goals.

Having the right mindset, coupled with a good solid plan, can get you going in the right direction. It will also help to keep you on the right track when things get difficult or you feel you are going off course.

Know Where You Are Now ☐
Have you compiled a list of accounts – brokerage and retirement?
Have you gathered copies of statements and organized in a notebook or in files?
Have you compiled a list of assets?
Have you compiled a list of liabilities?
Are you taking full advantage of your employer sponsored retirement plan?
Have you reviewed your current Social Security benefits (www.socialsecurity.gov/myaccount)
Are you ready to move forward?
Other?

Sources

1. Social Security Administration website can be reached by visiting (https://www.ssa.gov/pubs/EN-05-10024.pdf).

2. "How to plan for rising health care costs - Estimated cost for health care post-age 65? Try $285,000 per couple in assets needed today." Fidelity Viewpoints April 1, 2019. (https://www.fidelity.com/viewpoints/personal-finance/plan-for-rising-health-care-costs)

3. Ibid.

4. Genworth Cost of Care Survey 2018 can be viewed by visiting the following website at (https://www.genworth.com/aging-and-you/finances/cost-of-care.html)

5. Ibid.

6. Medicare.gov website can be reached by visiting (https://www.medicare.gov/your-medicare-costs/medicare-costs-at-a-glance)

Chapter 2: Know Where You Want to Go

In addition to knowing your assets and liabilities, it is important to focus on knowing where you want to go in retirement. Being able to retire will encompass deciding where you want to live, what type of activities you want to participate in and prioritizing those goals.

Remember that the accumulation of wealth is not an end but rather a means to accomplish your lifetime goals. You have to know your desired destinations or goals in order to develop an 'interactive road map' or 'GPS', for where you are headed. This is why it is so important to know where you want to go - and the GPS method can help you to establish your projected route. You can plan for what you need, based on where you are starting from right now, and also determine if and/or when you will need to make adjustments along the way.

A GPS For Your Retirement

I like to think of it as getting the big picture view from 30,000 feet so that you have a clear view of where you're going and can then plot a more detailed, step-by-step course on how to get yourself there. This entails assessing your investments, evaluating the need to downsize, seeking other potential sources of income and even knowing when it may be time to sell various assets. But without this type of planning, having just basic ideas of retirement are abstract. Once you make an actual plan, though, you will be much more assured of moving forward - and you'll also have the confidence that you can get there.

The GPS method starts with a "top down" approach. It takes a look first at the big picture overall, and then breaks it down into more specific individual strategies for what you need to do in order to get there. In some cases, you may have various "gaps" in your current plan - gaps that may otherwise have gone unnoticed without having a detailed projection for how to get you to all of your intended future goals. The GPS method finds those gaps, and helps you to fill them in.

How to Get There from Here - GPS Analogy

Have you ever planned a two-week long vacation to a place that was far away, but yet not looked at a map before you got in the car and started driving? Doubtful. It just simply wouldn't make any sense. How would you know where you were going - in fact, how would you even know which direction to start out?

Now, what about planning a twenty- to thirty-year vacation without first looking at a map of where you want to go? Sounds pretty silly doesn't it? But the reality is that many people "plan" for their retirement that way. Sure, they may be saving money for the future and they may even be setting aside a sizeable chunk in their employer sponsored retirement plan in an IRA account, and/or in personal savings and investments. But if you don't have a clear cut direction for where you want to end up, then how do you know if your investments are performing like they're supposed to be? In fact, how do you know if you're even invested in the right financial vehicles for you at all? The answer is that without a clear-cut plan in place, *you don't.*

Plan for the Destination

The beauty of creating your own roadmap is that no two journeys are exactly alike. The GPS method isn't a "cookie cutter" approach. Because retirement is such a unique journey for everyone, with this approach, you can decide where you want to go and how you want your future to look. Then, once you've determined your ultimate destination, the GPS method will help you to create a plan that will get you there. The GPS method takes into account assets including retirement and non-retirement, Social Security benefits, expected expenses, and income.

The way you spend your time in retirement will have a substantial impact on the future of your finances. The time to start planning for that is right now.

You've probably heard it said that most people will put more time towards planning a two-week vacation than they do planning their own retirement. But, by just taking an hour every couple of months to look at your GPS plan, you can see if your retirement projections are on track, and whether or not you need to make any adjustments. In fact, with the GPS method, once your plan has been set up, it takes very little time at all to keep the plan intact and running smoothly, ensuring that the financial vehicles you have chosen to take you to your destination are still performing as you had anticipated.

Projections Are the Key to Your Success

One of the most important things you can do when planning for retirement is a projection. I refer to it as a GPS for your retirement, because it will take you from where you are now to where you want to be in retirement. If you are trying to go somewhere you've never been before, you need a map...a GPS. The map, in this case, is a projection – there is no short cut– it is a must. You can conceptualize what you want your retirement to look like but if you want to know right now where you are, whether you need to work longer or whether you can retire sooner, you need a projection.

Alternatively, having an actual plan provides you with a way to not just know where you are going, but to actually set the course. Having your own personal GPS will also help to keep you on track so that you stay on course with your plan.

Once you have a projection prepared, it is important to review it annually to adjust for any changes that may have occurred in your life. Did your income increase? Have you experienced rising expenses? Is your mortgage paid off? How about your debt? Has that changed? All these things need to be addressed. Any changes will require an adjustment or recalculation of your plan. I don't believe there is any shortcut to successful retirement planning. If you take the time to get on course and adjust for changes along the way, you will transition into the retirement you have envisioned.

Below is a sample Retirement Summary created with the data provided on our GPS Questionnaire:

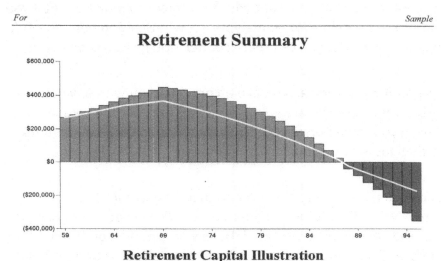

For   *Sample*

Retirement Summary

Retirement Capital Illustration

The analysis begins at your current age and extends through your life expectancy. It includes all assets, both tax advantaged and taxable, all expenses, including education funding if applicable, other income and expense estimates, defined benefit pensions, and Social Security benefits. The graph illustrates the growth and depletion of capital assets as seen in Retirement Capital Analysis. The line within the graph illustrates the value of future retirement assets in today's dollars.

General Assumptions:

Rates of Return Before and After Retirement Used in Illustration:		
Taxable RORs:	4%	4%
Tax Def. RORs:	4%	4%
Tax Free RORs:	4%	4%
Annuity RORs:	4%	4%

Retirement Spending Needs*	$36,000
Retirement Age	Sample - 70
Inflation - Current	2%
Inflation - Retirement	2%
Tax Rate - Current	20%
Tax Rate - Retirement	18%

* Spending needs are stated in today's after tax-dollars. See Assumptions page for complete listing of assumptions.

Actual future returns, taxes, expenses, and benefits are unknown. This illustration uses representative estimates and assumptions for educational and discussion purposes only. Do not rely on this report for investment analysis.

Retirement Capital Illustration Results:

It appears you may run out of money before the last life expectancy of age 95. The range of possible options you might consider to improve your situation include the following:

- Increase the rate of return on your investments.
- Increase your annual savings by $9,800/year ($817 month).
- Reduce your retirement spending needs by $6,300 to $29,700/year ($2,479/month).
- Defer your retirement by about 4 years.
- Combine any of the above and lower the requirements for each.

This report, and its hypothetical illustrations, are intended to form a basis for further discussion with your legal, accounting, and financial advisors. Actual future investment returns, taxes and inflation are unknown. Do not rely upon this report to predict future investment performance.

June 7, 2019   Page 6 of 15

22

The Retirement Summary takes into account wages, other income sources such as Social Security benefits, brokerage and retirement accounts, and expenses. In this case, the client's assets and income suffice through age 87 at which time the client then faces negative assets and income in retirement

Set Your Goals

People ask me all the time, "what is the best thing that I can do in order to prepare for retirement?" Although there are many things that can be done to prepare, I tell them that the very best thing is to develop a plan and then to work that plan consistently. The clearer your vision the better you will be able to develop your plan and set specific retirement goals.

One of the best ways to start setting your goals is to ask yourself what your ideal day would look like when you retire. For example, where will you be living? What will you do when you wake up? Who will you be surrounded by? What type of place will you be living in? All of these questions will help you in setting your retirement goals, and in turn, based on all of your answers, will also be important in determining how much savings or income you will need in order to accomplish them.

Where To Live

Where you want to live is probably the biggest consideration in knowing where you want to go.

Questions to ask yourself about where you want to live:

- Do you want to continue to live in your current area or do you want to move to another location?
- Does the current location or will a new location offer the conveniences you seek in retirement like proximity to family and friends, quality healthcare, preferred climate and resources to pursue your favorite activities?
- Do you want to stay in your current residence? If so, is it affordable in retirement? When answering this question, be sure to take into consideration maintenance costs, taxes, insurance costs, and improvement costs?
- Do you want a second residence where you can vacation? Again, consider the costs, maintenance, insurance, proximity to quality healthcare and activities?
- Do you want to downsize? Do you need the same size residence in retirement? If you downsize, can the savings that result further your retirement goals? For instance, will you be able to travel more, pursue expensive hobbies (e.g., buying a boat, motor home), or financially assist loved ones with education costs?

What To Do

An important second consideration is how will you keep active? This means, you must plan your time. As humans and former professionals, we expect structure in our lives; thrive with it but suffer without it.

Travel

Having the time to travel is what many retirees look forward to during retirement. How much you can travel depends on your personal financial situation. Even those with limited budgets find a way to meet their travel goals by traveling with a group. Some even make a plan that dramatically alters their lives. For instance, they may decide to sell their home and buy an RV. Get ready to pull out the passport and dust it off. Take that trip to Europe you've always wanted to take but never had the time to do. Or load up the car and drive across country like you and your spouse have always talked about doing. Just hit the open road (or sky) and see what the world has to offer.

Leisure activities

We all have activities that we enjoy doing in our spare time. Now that you have more of it, you can spend it doing leisure activities such as, golfing, playing tennis, hiking and biking for all the sports enthusiasts; camping and gardening for the naturalists; and reading and writing for the creatives. Whatever way you enjoy spending your time, now you can enjoy even more hours doing it.

Crafts/Hobby

For those with a love of crafting, retirement can become full-time arts and crafts time. Making handmade greeting cards, sewing, knitting, scrapbooking, building model trains, planes or automobiles. Whatever your craft or hobby pleasure, now you can spend more of your time doing what you love.

New career

Are you are retiring from a job that you've had more out of necessity than want? You've had to pay the bills and your job provided the means to meet those responsibilities. Maybe it wasn't the career of your dreams, but now is your chance to pursue your job that can make all your dreams com true. And if you've planned accordingly, the new job/career is more about satisfaction and expanding horizons, than money.

Start a business

Be your own boss. Retirement can be a great time to turn experiences and knowledge into your own business. Many companies actively recruit retirees to provide them with consulting services. A hobby is often the impetus to a new business. You may consider buying and opening a franchise. Franchises already have the licensing, rules, regulations, marketing, strategies, and plans figured out for you. Many offer financing so you don't have to deplete your savings or sell investments to come up with the start-up money.

Volunteer

If you prefer to do something meaningful with your time but don't need or want to be paid, consider volunteering. Every community in the country has numerous volunteer opportunities available. Volunteering is a doubly fulfilling because it makes you feel good to help those in need and to contribute to a cause you feel strongly about. Call local organizations, charities, schools, hospitals, and/ or churches to find out what type of volunteer opportunities are available.

Part-time employment

Maybe you still need to earn a little money on top of your retirement income, or you just want to work out of the home for a few hours a day or a couple days a week. Consider taking a part-time job which provides the opportunity to work in a new industry or even in your old industry. It helps to keep you active, allows you to exercise your brain and gives you a little extra spending money. And some part-time jobs, like Starbucks' baristas, not only receive part-time pay, but employee benefits as well.

Education

Pursuing additional education in retirement is a burgeoning sector. Colleges and universities around the country offer a myriad of courses geared toward seniors. The focus is on knowledge not necessarily earning credits and a degree. These types of programs often offer flexible class scheduling, an opportunity to socialize and a less formal setting to exchange ideas.

Prioritize Long Term And Short-Term Goals

Depending on how well you have saved for retirement and when you plan to retire you may need to prioritize your "know where you want to go" goals as long- term versus short-term. Your GPS retirement tracking system will provide you with a "map" for those goals. Generally long-term goals require five or more years to attain.

Typically, long-term goals include purchasing a vacation home, paying off debt and accumulating enough assets to live off the income generated. If, for example, one of your long-term goals is to purchase a home by the beach, then short-term goal is to save a certain amount of money each month or year as necessary.

Short-term goals, on the other hand, are those that may only take a year or less to achieve and include saving for the down payment on a new car, a small renovation or update to your home and funding your IRA.

Find balance in your life

Retirement doesn't have to mean full-time devotion to any one activity. It is a time for you to find life balance. A time for you to spend time doing what you enjoy—finding balance in your life between what you enjoy doing and taking care of your responsibilities at the same time. And it may be that one of the activities listed above or some combination of these activities help you to achieve this balance.

Make Healthy Life Choices

Enjoying your retirement years to its fullest is not just about having enough money to cover your living expenses either. Your retirement will be more enjoyable if your mind and body are in good health. Keeping your mind and body active, spending time with people you care about, and doing things you enjoy all contribute to a retirement worth living. As a boomer, you're expected to live longer than any generation before you, which means there are things you have to take into consideration about your health that no other generations had to think about.

Research has shown that both exercise and social contact contribute to longevity and can significantly improve your quality of life. So, take a walk, or better yet, organize a walking club. Volunteer for causes for which you have a passion. Start a small business. Challenge yourself by learning something you've always been curious about, whether it's origami or flying down the slopes on a snowboard with the grandkids. Disconnect the tube and curl up with a good book or spend hours chatting with a friend.

Guilt-free

Our GPS projection can provide the parameters for you to feel comfortable with fulfilling your goals and getting you where you want to go. If planned properly retirement need not be a time of frugality, but one filled with newness and purpose.

Having a clear vision can help you to be more confident about setting and successfully achieving your retirement destination. In addition, having this clarity will also help to reduce any anxiety that you may have about taking that important step from relying on your employer for income, to relying on yourself.

Programming your goals into your GPS can provide you with a specific track to run on and it will let you know if or when you have gone off course. This can make it much easier to re-route so that your goals can be accomplished rather than waiting until it is too late.

Know Where You Want to Go   ☐
Have you completed the GPS Questionnaire enclosed with the book?
Have you returned the completed GPS Questionnaire to Mahoney Asset Management?
Have you identified and set goals?
Have you decided where you want to live?
Have you planned how you will spend your time?
Have you prioritized your long- and short- term goals?
Other?

Chapter 3: Have A Plan

Have Purpose

A successful retirement will include knowing your sense of purpose.

Many people may not initially realize what an adjustment it can be adapting to a new routine, especially if that routine doesn't involve setting an alarm clock and commuting to and from work five or more days a week. It can be quite difficult to adjust from doing something you've been doing for many years – from a job, to raising children, to a new phase of life with more freedom and fewer constraints.

It is commonly believed that those who do not have adequate financial means would be much happier if they had more money to be able to have and do the things that they want. While wealth can tend to improve your overall sense of well-being there are some other key factors that also matter.

According to Keith Bender, economic expert at the University of Aberdeen, there are two other primary criteria that can have an even larger effect on your overall fulfillment in retirement than just money alone. These include your health and the reason for your retiring in the first place. Investing in your health is equally, if not, more important than financial well-being, as is having purpose after retirement.[1]

Research at the Sloan Center on Aging & Work at Boston College shows there is a type of "honeymoon" period at the beginning of retirement. After this time, there is often a period of realization that without a sense of purpose, this newfound freedom may not be enough. Having a sense of purpose is not only fulfilling, it improves one's overall happiness and can increase one's longevity.

David Buettner, a writer and explorer, has spent the bulk of his life traveling the world in search of answers. In his 2008 book, "The Blue Zones: Lessons for Living Longer From the People Who've Lived the Longest", Buettner interviewed centenarians from around the world in order to determine why they thought they had lived so long. He found that in every culture there is the notion of "ikigai" – a Japanese concept which means having a reason to get up in the morning and having a purpose. Buettner also found that people are the happiest when they spend their time and money on experiences as opposed to objects.[2]

According to a recent study published at the JAMA Network Open, "a growing body of literature suggests that having a strong sense of purpose in life leads to improvements in both physical and mental health and enhances overall quality of life." People who didn't have a strong life purpose, which is defined as "a self-organizing life aim that stimulates goals," were more likely to die than those who did, and specifically more likely to die of cardiovascular diseases.[3]

If you are struggling with what it is that you truly want to spend the next phase of your life doing, there are some questions that you can ask yourself in order to get you started down the right path.

These include:

- What are your key ideals and/or priorities?
- If you were to pass away tomorrow what would be your top 5 biggest regrets?
- If you were able to start your life over, but already knowing all that you know right now, what, if anything, would you do differently?

- Who in this world matters the most to you, and likewise, who are you important to?
- When you reflect back on your life what were you the happiest doing and why?
- What are some activities and / or hobbies that you enjoy doing?
- If you could stop doing anything in your life what would those things include?
- What are your key skills and talents?

Take your time to thoughtfully answer these questions. Writing down detailed responses will help you clarify how you see yourself in this phase of life and retirement. Once you have identified what is purposeful to you it will only become meaningful and enjoyable when acted upon.

For example, perhaps you once had an interest in photography, but time and budget constraints precluded you from pursuing it. Now, in retirement, is your opportunity to pursue that interest. In terms of being purposeful, your interest in photography is in itself meaningful to you as it brings enjoyment to you. And, if you decide to share your interest and proficiency by volunteering to photograph a charity event, the "purposefulness" then expands to include and benefit others.

A Meaningful Life

Exploring purpose in life and retirement is ongoing and dynamic. It requires evaluating and re-evaluating where you are in life and reflecting on your relationships, your environment and your health. Having and pursuing purpose is not about perfection either, it is about meaning and enjoyment.

Have A Plan   ☐
What is meaningful to you?
What are your talents and skills?
How do you see yourself giving back to family, friends and community?
What can you do to make your life and the lives of others more meaningful?
Passions
Purpose In Life letter

Sources

1. Bender, K. A. (2012). An analysis of well-being in retirement: The role of pensions, health, and "voluntariness" of retirement. The Journal of Socio-Economics, 41(4), 424–433. https://doi.org/10.1016/j.socec.2011.05.010

2. "How to 'Thrive': Dan Buettner's Secrets of Happiness." NPR Books. (http://www.npr.org/2010/11/28/131571885/how-to-thrive-dan-buettner-s-secrets-of-happiness)

3. "Association Between Life Purpose and Mortality Among US Adults Older Than 50 Years." (https://jamanetwork.com/journals/jamanetworkopen/fullarticle/2734064?utm_source=For_The_Media&utm_medium=referral&utm_campaign=ftm_links&utm_term=052419)

Chapter 4: Protect Yourself And Your Assets Through Insurance

In retirement, you not only need to ensure that you have enough income for your expenses, but it is essential that you protect the income and assets you have accumulated. Otherwise, you could find yourself dipping into your savings or worse, putting items on credit should an emergency, health issue, or other potentially costly, unplanned event occur.

Insurance can help to protect things like your home, your vehicle, and other tangible items, as well as the intangibles, like the high cost of healthcare. You can even insure income to last for a certain number of years, or for the remainder of your entire lifetime, regardless of how long that may be.

Healthcare and Baby Boomers

According to the US Census Bureau, baby boomers (those born between 1944 and 1964) number 74 million people. In 2050, the population aged 65 and over is projected to be 83.7 million people, which is almost double its estimated population of 43.1 million people in 2012. The baby boomers are largely responsible for this increase in the older population, as they began turning 65 in 2011. The aging of the population will have wide-ranging implications for the country. The projected growth of the older population in the United States will present challenges to policy makers and programs, such as Social Security and Medicare. It will also affect families, businesses, and health care providers.

Medicare.com identified the following top five health concerns among baby boomers:

1. Alzheimer's
2. Diabetes
3. Flu and Pneumonia
4. Heart Disease
5. Obesity

As part of your retirement planning you will want to assess the state of your current health as well as potential health concerns going forward. As healthcare expenses continue to rise it can be devastating to your resources unless you have some type of insurance to protect yourself.

You will want to consider private insurance, long-term care insurance, Medicare Part B, Medicare Supplemental and Medicare Part D. You may also profit from understanding the various Medicaid tricks, traps, and troubles which have bankrupted many a family when one member needed nursing home care.

Health Insurance

Health insurance is not an option for most individuals, it is a necessity. While working, most employees have health coverage provided through their employer but once retired the employer paid premiums, low co-payments, and cheap out-of-pocket expenses may get thrown out the window. Unless your employer covers your health insurance in retirement (which most do not), then you need to consider what options of health care coverage are available to you.

There are many health insurance plans to choose from, each with its own features and exclusions. The older you get the harder it can be to get health insurance coverage. Once you retire, the sooner you can obtain health coverage the better off you will be when it comes to the costs, terms, and conditions of the coverage. Of course, your health will be a major, determining factor that can and will impact your ability to obtain coverage as well as the associated costs.

Considerations of Coverage

There are five main considerations of coverage you need to be concerned with when shopping for a health insurance plan:

1. Major medical coverage
2. Choice of health care providers
3. Lifetime maximum benefits
4. Deductibles and co-pay
5. Guaranteed renewals

Major Medical

Major medical coverage is your primary concern, because it is the most expensive part of health care and without it you can strain, if not drain, your resources. This is particularly true if you have a major accident or are diagnosed with a serious illness. This type of coverage includes hospital stays, visits to the doctor, X-rays, and laboratory work.

Doctors and Specialists

A second consideration is your ability to choose the doctors and specialists you want. Depending on the source of your insurance, private and/or governmental, you will want to ensure the doctor or specialist is "in-network" or covered by the plan. Some plans allow for doctors "out of network" at additional cost to you.

Lifetime Maximum Benefits

The third consideration is lifetime maximum benefits. This is the total amount of coverage that is paid out over the life of the policy. Ideally, you want to choose a plan that has a maximum lifetime benefit of $5 million or does not have a maximum limit at all just in case you have a scenario with a major illness or accident.

Deductibles and Co Payments

Fourth, you need to consider deductibles and co-payments. These two items have a direct effect on the premium of the policy, so the higher the amount of the deductible and the higher the amount of the co-payments, the lower the monthly premium payments. The best way to keep your health insurance premiums affordable is to choose a plan with the highest deductible and co-payments you can afford.

Guaranteed Renewal

Finally, you may want to seek out a plan that has a guaranteed renewal feature. This feature allows for the policy to continuously renew, unless cancelled, regardless of your health condition and without having to take a physical exam. As we age and become more susceptible to illness, the guaranteed renewal feature extends protection at a time when it is needed most.

Purchasing a Plan

So where is the best place for you to buy a health insurance plan? You have several options when shopping for a health insurance provider.

Affordable Care Act

In 2010, President Obama signed into law the Affordable Care Act ("ACA") providing affordable health insurance to more people. Under the ACA everyone is eligible for healthcare coverage including those with pre-existing conditions.

The federal government and state governments offer "marketplaces" for individuals, families and small businesses to compare health plan options. The federal government website, https://www.healthcare.gov, provides detailed information on enrollment along with links to various state websites offering plan options depending on your needs.

It should be noted that under the ACA, for plan years through 2018, you may have had to pay a fee called the individual Shared Responsibility Payment when you filed your federal taxes. The reason you were required to pay this fee is because you could afford health insurance but elected not to buy it. Starting with the 2019 plan year, the Shared Responsibility Payment no longer applied. While the penalty no longer applied in 2019 at the federal level, certain states did assess a penalty if you do not have health coverage.[3]

Health Insurance Agents

A second option is to contact health insurance agents. Health insurance agents represent one or more health insurance companies and can help you choose the providers and services that are best for your needs.

Health Insurance Companies

A third option is to go directly to the health insurance companies and shop and compare the policies yourself. Doing it yourself can be time consuming and confusing if you are not familiar with how insurance policies work.

Employer Provided Coverage

If you haven't retired and you have employer provided health insurance, you will want to find out if the coverage will or can extend into your retirement. If you are self-employed and have insurance coverage, talk with your provider to find out how your retirement and/or closing your business (if applicable) will affect your coverage. If coverage terminates once you retire (whether employed by a company or self-employed), you will need to pursue your options to replace it.

Coverage After Age 65 - Medicare

For those who are already retired or are 65 or older, the government offers a health insurance plan known as, Medicare.

Medicare has four major parts of enrollment:
1. Part A: Hospital expenses
2. Part B: Physician and other expenses
3. Part C: Supplemental coverage (third party insurer)
4. Part D: Prescription drug coverage

Part A Medicare coverage is automatic once you apply for Medicare. Parts B, C, and D are optional. With Medicare coverage, you are responsible for meeting deductibles and paying co-payments for Medicare services. To bridge the gap there is also Medigap insurance which may cover the charges Medicare does not. If you cannot afford to pay for the deductible and co-payments because of low income, Medicaid is available to help people in this situation. Medicaid is a state funded insurance plan and can also be used with Medigap insurance.

Part D coverage is relatively new, having started in 2006. It helps to cover the cost of prescription drugs. A monthly premium is paid to an insurance carrier which allows you to use the insurance carrier's network of pharmacies to purchase your prescription medications. Instead of paying full price, you will pay a copay or percentage of the drug's cost. The insurance company will pay the rest.[4]

There are restrictions to Part D you need to consider before opting in. For example, certain medications may not be covered, only generic medications may be covered without a doctor's request for non-generic brands. Prior authorization for certain medications may also be required.

There are also enrollment restrictions with Part D, so be sure to make an educated decision before opting out. If you choose not to enroll in Part D when you apply for Medicare, but decide to enroll later, there is a penalty fee charged. A better option may be to enroll in the lowest cost Part D option available, if necessary, and then upgrade to a better coverage option later, to avoid paying the penalty.

For complete Medicare information, visit www.medicare.gov.

Secondary Health Insurance

Supplementing your Medicare benefits may be necessary to ensure that you are covered once you retire. Check with your employer before you retire to see if you are eligible for health care benefits during retirement—these benefits can act as a secondary or supplemental insurance to Medicare. Supplemental insurance will assist you by closing the gap between what Medicare will pay and what you must pay out of pocket. If your employer does not provide coverage after retirement it is strongly recommended you consult with an experienced, licensed insurance agent about supplemental insurance.

Long-Term Care Insurance

Once you have your health plan coverage established, you may think the battle is over and sigh in relief. Many retirees worry whether or not to buy long-term care insurance ("LTC") which covers extended stays in nursing homes. These policies are very expensive, with many exclusions and limitations, which is why the decision to buy or not buy plagues many people.

You may think that long term care insurance is too expensive but not having it can be much more expensive if you eventually need it. According to SeniorLiving.org the national average cost for nursing home care is between $89,297 and $100,375, although the cost can vary greatly among geographical regions.[1] By comparison, an article by Liz Weston on the website www.nerdwallet.com reports the national average long term care insurance premium for a 55 year old couple was about $3,050 in 2019.[2] Significant premium increases can be expected if you wait until age 65 to purchase a policy.

You will need to take into consideration whether or not an long term care policy will benefit you. For most, the length of stay in a nursing home is less than one year which means the cost of a policy far exceeds the cost of paying for a one-year stay out of your own pocket. Most individuals have family or friends who can care for them during this one year, which means they avoid the nursing-home stay altogether.

Medicare does not usually cover expenses associated with long term care, it picks up the cost for the first 100 days of a stay in a nursing home as long as certain conditions are met. Medicaid might cover long term care expenses, but it generally doesn't kick in unless you're impoverished or until you've "spent down" your assets to the level required in your state. When you apply, Medicaid has the right to look back at all your financial transactions over the preceding 60 months to discover whether you gave away your assets or sold them for less than fair market value to qualify for benefits. If so, you could be ineligible for full Medicaid benefits for up to 100 months.

If one does need long term care, the costs associated with long term care, without coverage, can consume hard earned assets and place a burden on loved ones not only financially but also emotionally.

Ultimately, your decision boils down to paying long term care costs yourself or transferring some of the financial risk to an insurance company through a long term care policy. Choosing the long term care insurance policy that's appropriate for you involves a number of variables, including your age, health and financial status. By understanding all your options, you'll be better equipped to make an informed decision regarding your long-term care needs.

Make sure that part of your financial investment portfolio is devoted to covering medical expenses during retirement. Knowing what private insurance, supplemental insurance and Medicare offers and which option or combination of options is best for you is a "must do" part of retiring planning.

Ideally, the best way to save on healthcare costs is to live a healthy life and avoid medical costs altogether. Illnesses like diabetes and heart disease can kill a lot of healthcare dollars over your lifetime. Exercise, eat a healthy diet, don't smoke and drink alcohol in moderation. Do what you can to prevent health problems down the road.

Life Insurance

Prior to retirement most people purchase life insurance as protection against loss of income especially if two incomes support the family lifestyle and/or there are minor children. After retirement, protection of employment income and children are less of an issue but that does not mean you should not have life insurance.

In addition to providing financial gain to beneficiaries, proceeds from a life policy can be used to pay off debt such as credit card or mortgage, can supplement social security or pension income, can pay estate or inheritance taxes and can serve as a source for charitable contributions.

Types of Life Insurance

Term Life

Term life insurance is as it implies; it is for a certain period. Term polices are generally issued for periods of 10, 20, or 30 years. If you pass away during the selected period, the insurance company will pay out the death benefit to your beneficiaries listed on the policy.

Whole Life

Whole life provides coverage for one's lifetime. The period of coverage spans from the time of purchase until death. The policy includes a component called cash value. The cash value component grows tax deferred and you can borrow against the policy in the form of a loan. If you do not repay the loan, the cash value at the time of death will be reduced. You can also cancel or surrender the policy for the cash value. Keep in mind that the cash value component makes the premiums for a whole life policy higher than term insurance.

Guaranteed Universal Life

Another type of life insurance, highly recommended for seniors who are purchasing for the first time, is guaranteed universal life ("GUL"). GUL offers coverage until you reach a certain age, such as 90, 95, 100. This age parameter is unlike term insurance, which offers coverage for a certain period. In addition, level premiums and death benefits are guaranteed as long as the premiums are paid on time.

Group Life with Employer

If you are part of a group life insurance plan with your employer, you will want to determine if you can continue or convert the plan to an individual plan.

Annuities

In addition to traditional forms of insurance policies, like life and healthcare, there are annuity policies. An annuity is a contract between one or two individuals and an insurance company. This contract can guarantee a stream of income to the person, known as the annuitant. The annuitant's age will determine the amount of a lump sum deposit or periodic deposits that are made over time. Growth of the value of the annuity is market driven and is tax deferred until it is either paid out as income or it is withdrawn.

Types of annuities available in the market include:

- **Fixed Annuities** - Fixed annuities offer the policy holder a fixed amount of interest that is credited on an annual basis. This rate is declared by the insurance carrier that offers the annuity. The key benefit to owning a fixed annuity is the safety of principal that it provides.

- **Variable Annuities** - Variable annuities are set up in a similar manner as fixed annuities, however, these vehicles allow the policy holder to participate in market appreciation via a number of different investment options. These underlying investments are typically held in "sub-accounts" in the form of mutual funds. Those who own variable annuities have the opportunity to grow the value of the account based on market performance. They are also subject to downward market risk.

- **Indexed Annuities** - An indexed annuity is a type of annuity that has its return linked to an underlying market index such as the S&P 500 or the DJIA (Dow Jones Industrial Average). The owner of an indexed annuity is not actually purchasing shares in the investment, but rather interest is credited to their account based on changes in the index to which the annuity is linked.

One appealing characteristic of an annuity is the income stream that it can provide. This is one reason why annuities are purchased by those who are retired or those who are approaching retirement. It should be noted that withdrawing funds from an annuity prior to its surrender free date may negatively impact the amount of guaranteed income.

In addition to a regular, guaranteed stream of income, annuities often offer additional benefits such as a long-term care and/or nursing home rider (an insurance policy provision that adds benefits to or amends the terms of a basic insurance policy), which allows the policy holder to withdraw funds to cover their long-term care and/or nursing home expenses without incurring surrender charges.

Upon death of the policy holder, the insurance company will payout proceeds to designated beneficiaries in a lump sum or periodic payments.

The Bottom Line

When you were younger with young children and a mortgage your need for life insurance was very high especially as a safeguard against an untimely death. Now that you're older, your children are self-sufficient and your mortgage is paid off, the need for life insurance may be less necessary and those life insurance premiums may be better spent on long term care insurance or investments that will support you and your loved ones during retirement and thereafter.

Safeguarding your health and your assets through insurance is an essential part of planning for retirement. Because of the myriad of options available it is best to speak with a professional who can help define your needs and procure the necessary coverage, while at the same time weighing the costs of coverage against those needs.

Protect Yourself And Your Assets Through Insurance

☐

Have you reviewed your health insurance options? including private, Medicare and supplemental?
Have you considered if Long Term Care for you?
Have you reviewed life insurance policies to ensure it meets your needs?
Have you reviewed life insurance policies to ensure the beneficiary designations are current?
Other?

Sources

1. https://www.seniorliving.org/nursing-homes/costs

2. https://www.nerdwallet.com/article/investing/long-term-care

Chapter 5: Understand The Impact Of Taxes

Taxes are a part of our lives, retired or not. In addition to sales taxes and property taxes, taxes generated from supplemental income (e.g., income from rental properties), investments and monetary gifts need to be considered when planning for retirement.

Federal Tax Brackets

Depending on your level of income, you will currently fall into one of seven different tax brackets.

Federal tax brackets for 2019 are as follows:

2019 Federal Tax Bracket Thresholds Taxable Income by Filing Status				
Marginal tax rate	Single	Married filing jointly and surviving spouse	Head of household	Married filing separately
10%	$0–$9,700	$0–$19,400	$0–$13,850	$0–$9,700
12%	$9,701–$39,475	$19,401–$78,950	$13,851–$52,850	$9,701–$39,475
22%	$39,476–$84,200	$78,951–$168,400	$52,851–$84,200	$39,476–$84,200
24%	$84,201–$160,725	$168,401–$321,450	$84,201–$160,700	$84,201–$160,725
32%	$160,726–$204,100	$321,451–$408,200	$160,701–$204,100	$160,726–$204,100
35%	$204,101–$510,300	$408,201–$612,350	$204,101–$510,300	$204,101–$306,175
37%	$510,301 and more	$612,351 and more	$510,301 and more	$306,176 and more

Source: https://www.creditkarma.com/tax/i/2019-tax-brackets-things-to-know

Currently, the highest income tax bracket is 37%. Because brackets have changed over the years, it could be that by the time you retire there may be income tax brackets that are in excess of 40%.

Calculating The Tax Due for a Single in 2019:

Filing status: Single	
Taxable income (TI)	**Income tax due**
$0–$9,700	10% of taxable income
$9,701–$39,475	$970 + 12% of Total Income over $9,700
$39,476–$84,200	$4,543 + 22% of Total Income over $39,475
$84,201–$160,725	$14,382.50 + 24% of Total Income over $84,200
$160,726–$204,100	$32,748.50 + 32% of Total Income over $160,725
$204,101–$510,300	$46,628.50 + 35% of Total Income over $204,100
$510,301 and more	$153,798.50 + 37% of Total Income over $510,300

Source: https://www.creditkarma.com/tax/i/2019-tax-brackets-things-to-know

Using 2019 figures, the lowest tax bracket is 10% for single filers with income between $0 and $9,700. If you fall into this category you will owe 10% of that income in tax. If you earn any more than that amount not every single dollar of the money that you earn may be taxed at that same percentage.

As an example, if you earn $100 more than $9,700, or a total of $9,800, you will owe 10% tax on the money that falls into the first bracket. So, you will owe 10% on the first $9,700 that you earned (10% X $9,700 = $970.00 in tax).

But then you will also owe 12% on that $100 amount that has spilled over into the next bracket. Income in the next bracket is taxed at 12%. Therefore, the additional $100 that you earn will be taxed at 12%, so you will owe $12 on those earnings ($100 X 12% = $12 in tax). In total for the year, your taxes will be $982.00 ($970.00 + $12 = $982.00).

Taxes on Withdrawals

The type of account from which you withdraw income will be a key factor because the tax assessment will differ depending on the type of account.

Tax Deferred Accounts

Money withdrawn from tax-deferred accounts, such as 401(k)s and traditional IRAs, will be taxed as ordinary income. If you contributed to these types of accounts with pre-tax dollars then 100% of your withdrawal will be taxed at your ordinary income rate because these dollars have not previously been taxed.

If you receive income from a defined benefit pension plan and/or from a government pension the income is typically taxed at your ordinary income tax rate (provided you did not make any after-tax contributions into the plan).

Roth IRAs Accounts

Roth IRA accounts, on the other hand, are funded with contributions "after-tax" which means you cannot deduct the amount of the contribution from your salary like you would with a 401(k)-employer retirement plan. Growth of the value of a Roth IRA is tax-free as are withdrawals as long as the Roth account is at least five years in existence, and you are at least 59 ½ when taking a withdrawal.

Brokerage Accounts

When you withdraw money from a non-retirement account (commonly referred to as a brokerage account) in the form of profits from the sale of stocks, mutual funds, or bonds, the withdrawn money is taxed at the "capital gain" rate. Short term capital gains (held for less than a year) are taxed at your ordinary tax rate whereas long term capital gains (held for more than a year) are taxed at 0%, 15% and 20%, depending on your income. Long term capital tax rates are usually lower than short term tax rates. These lower taxes rates serve as an incentive to invest longer term.

Annuities

Many people also receive income from annuities in retirement. The tax on withdrawals from a non-retirement annuity will depend on whether or not the funds withdrawn are from gains (e.g., profit) or principal (the amount of money you invested in the annuity). Funds withdrawn from principle will be tax free while funds withdrawn from gains will be taxed at your ordinary income tax rate.

On the other hand, if you have an annuity purchased with pre-tax dollars, such as with an annuity purchased in an IRA account, then any withdrawal is considered income to you and taxable at your ordinary tax rate.

Social Security

Social Security income can be taxable. This usually happens only if you have other substantial income, such as, but not limited to, wages, interest income and dividends.

You will pay tax on only 85 percent of your Social Security benefits, based on Internal Revenue Service (IRS) rules. If you:

- File a federal tax return as an "individual" and your combined income is:
    - Between $25,000 and $34,000, you may have to pay income tax on up to 50 percent of your benefits.
    - More than $34,000, up to 85 percent of your benefits may be taxable.
- File a joint return, and you and your spouse have a combined income that is:
    - Between $32,000 and $44,000, you may have to pay income tax on up to 50 percent of your benefits.
    - More than $44,000, up to 85 percent of your benefits may be taxable.
- Are married and file a separate tax return, you probably will pay taxes on your benefits.

(Your adjusted gross income + Nontaxable interest + ½ of your Social Security benefits = Your "combined income").

Each January, Social Security Benefit statements are issued showing the amount of benefits received in the previous year. The statement can help determine if benefits received are subject to taxation.[1]

Work With Professionals

It's not necessarily what you earn but what you keep. Having to hand over a certain amount of your income in taxes during retirement will obviously have an effect on how much you will actually net to be used for paying your living expenses. Working with a qualified financial advisor and tax preparer can help to understand and budget for the impact taxes will have on your retirement income, particularly when you need to withdraw money and need to determine which sources will incur less of a tax consequence.

Understand The Impact Of Taxes ☐

Do you know what type of accounts you own? IRA? Annuity?
Do you know which income sources are taxable?
Do you know your current tax rate?
Have you met with a qualified tax professional?
Other?

Sources

1. https://www.ssa.gov/planners/taxes.html

Chapter 6: Plan Ahead - Estate Planning

Even for those who don't consider themselves to be wealthy, estate planning provides the opportunity to designate, among other things, those to whom you would like to leave financial or personal possessions to, those who can act on your behalf and those who will act as guardian for minors.

Other considerations include:
- Planning for the succession of a business.
- Providing for those with special needs who receive government assistance or for those who poorly manage money and/or their lives.
- Having insurance to provide for survivors, funeral expenses and debt.

When it comes to basic estate planning there are a few documents everyone should have.

Wills

The first item on your list should be a will. A will is defined as being a "legally enforceable declaration of how an individual wants his or her assets to be distributed upon their death."[1]

A person who dies without a valid will is said to have died "intestate." When this occurs the distribution of property and assets are left up to the government and in some cases, property and assets can end up property of the state. If you don't create a will your state of residency will essentially create one for you, and it probably won't distribute your assets in the way that you would have liked them to be distributed.

Of great importance when preparing a will is designating an executor. The executor or administrator is responsible for managing the distribution of your assets until completed, which amounts to the payment of debts/expenses and filing of tax return(s). The executor should be one or more persons, and/or an entity (e.g., bank) that you trust to fulfill the role.

In addition to distribution of assets, a will provides the forum to designate the guardianship of minors and dependents. These designations satisfy your directives with regard to your remains. They also alleviate tensions among competing loved ones who believe to know what is best for you.

Numerous websites offer instructions and documentation to prepare a will. A "do-it-yourself" will may be legitimate but the preparation of a legally binding will by a qualified estate attorney will bring greater peace of mind. At a minimum, a "do-it-yourself" will need the valid signature of the "will-maker" along with the signatures of two witnesses.

Power of attorney

A power of attorney gives one or more persons the power to act on your behalf as your agent. The power may be limited to a particular activity, such as closing the sale of your home. Or the power granted may be more diverse by granting the power to handle all personal, financial, and business transactions. The power may give temporary or permanent authority to act on your behalf. The power may take effect immediately, or only upon the occurrence of a future event, such as the time it is determined that you are unable to act for yourself due to mental or physical disability.[2]

If you do not have a power of attorney and become unable to manage your personal or business affairs, it may become necessary for a court to appoint one or more people to act for you. Depending on your local state, people appointed in this manner are referred to as guardians, conservators, or committees. If a court proceeding, sometimes known as intervention, is needed, you may not have the ability to choose the person who will act for you. Few people want to be subject to a public proceeding in this manner so being proactive to designate a power of attorney and defining their "powers" is very important.[2]

Living Will

A living will describes and instructs how an individual would or would not wish his or her end-of-life care to be managed.

A living will serves as an advance directive that takes effect when an individual is considered to be terminally ill, seriously injured, or near the end of their life. Advance directives are written instructions regarding medical care decisions to be made by an appointed person(s) if you are unable to communicate such decisions yourself. Not only does a living will allow you to dictate your medical care when you are unable to, it can also relieve your loved ones or guardians of having to make difficult decisions at a time of crisis.

Letter of Intention

A letter of intention, while not legally binding, is a practical and personal way to leave information and instructions. It may include specifics about what to do with your remains. It also details the type of memorial service you will have, if any, and who you would like certain possessions to go to. It may be more general in nature and include people that have you have shared memories or those that you have been intimate with over the course of your life. Or a combination of both.

Revocable Living Trust

A revocable living trust is established in writing and involves the trustmaker, the trustee, and the beneficiary. In a typical situation, when the trust agreement is created these three people will be the same person. Once the trust agreement is signed, the trustmaker funds the trust with his or her assets and designates the trust itself as the beneficiary of retirement accounts, life insurance, annuities and any other assets. The trustee then manages, invests, and spends the trust property for the benefit of the beneficiary.

Because the trustmaker doesn't own any of the trust property in his or her own name—assets are owned by the trustee for the benefit of the beneficiary--when the trustmaker dies, the trust assets can be transferred without going through the probate process. Even though the trustmaker has died, the trust itself continues to live on and the successor trustee, who is named in the trust agreement, has the legal authority to step into the trustmaker's shoes to collect life insurance proceeds, retirement accounts, annuities, and other assets. The successor trustee then pays all of the trustmaker's final bills, debts and taxes, and distributes the balance of the trust funds to the trustmaker's ultimate beneficiaries—also named in the trust agreement

Probate

The process of administering an estate, whether or not a will is involved, is called probate. The process will be prolonged if there is no will as it requires a court to designate a representative, an accounting of all assets and a determination of who are legitimate heirs or beneficiaries.

It is preferable to avoid probate not only because the process of administering an estate can be very lengthy but also because most states assess probate fees which can be as high as 5% of the estate value, if not higher. In addition to probate fees there are attorney fees, court fees, appraisal fees and accountant fees to consider.

Assets which designate a specific beneficiary bypass the probate process. Assets which bypass the process include retirement accounts like IRAs and 401(k)s, insurance products like life insurance and annuities, jointly held accounts (as the assets transfer to the surviving joint owner), and certain trusts like a revocable living trust. It is imperative to review beneficiary designations on a regular basis to ensure the designations are accurately titled and those named are in line with who you would like to receive the asset. Also, it should be noted that designating your "estate" as a beneficiary negates avoiding probate as the assets so designated will transfer to your estate.

Estate Taxes

While we're all familiar with the taxes that we pay throughout our lives, in some cases, there can also be a big tax bill due upon death. This is what is known as an estate tax.

The IRS defines estate taxes as being "a tax on your right to transfer property at your death." It consists of an accounting of everything that you own or have certain interests in at your death. The property included may consist of cash and securities, real estate, insurance, trusts, annuities, business interests and other assets.[3]

Although most estates typically don't require the filing of an estate tax return, estate returns are required for estates that have combined gross assets, which include prior taxable gifts that exceed a certain amount. For 2019, that amount is $11.4 million.[2] The federal estate tax rate on estates that exceed this amount is 40%, which can reduce one's estate significantly unless prior planning has taken place. In terms of American wealth, only the estates of the wealthiest 0.2 percent owe any estate tax.

All Situations Are Different

Because all situations are different it is important to consider putting together a "team" including a qualified estate planning attorney, a certified accountant with tax estate planning experience and a licensed financial advisor to ensure all your financial, health and personal directives are carried out according to your wishes.

Effective estate planning requires regular reviews taking place every one to three years. It is strongly recommended that all important documents, as well as insurance policies, and retirement account beneficiary designations, are reviewed and updated regularly as situations change. For instance, death of a spouse or child may affect the directive in a will or a trust. Likewise, divorce or death of a spouse may impact who is named beneficiary of retirement accounts, insurance policies and/or investment accounts.

Along with copies of one's will and insurance policies, copies of current bank and investment statements, deeds, titles, information to contact advisors, lawyers, accountants, etc. should be organized and in one place for easy accessibility.

Plan Ahead - Estate Planning ☐
Do you have a will?
Is your will current?
Do you need to update your will?
Do you have a power of attorney? Is it current?
Do you have a living will or healthcare proxy?
Have you prepared a letter of intention?
Have you met with a qualified estate/eldercare attorney?
Other?

Sources

1. https://www.investopedia.com/terms/w/will.asp

2. https://www.americanbar.org/groups/real_property_trust_est
   ate/resources/estate_planning/power_of_attorney/

3. www.IRS.gov (https://www.irs.gov/Businesses/Small-
   Businesses-&-Self-Employed/Estate-Tax)

Chapter 7: Recognize Market Risks

With any journey there will be risks along the way. If you are unaware of these risks or you haven't properly prepared for them, reaching your goals and objectives may be compromised.

For those who anticipate the potential risks the bumps along the road will seem like a normal part of the trip.

Important risks to understand include:

Market Risk

One of the biggest risks is market risk. The constant ups and downs of the stock market means you will need to protect what you have saved. Even a slight market "correction" can essentially wipe out years of what you have worked for and accumulated.

Markets are at risk when major events occur such as political unrest or uncertainty, interest rate fluctuations, natural disasters and recessions.

At a minimum, protection of principal (the amount of money invested) is the goal of most investors. This is especially true for anyone who may have lost money in the market downturn of 2008. Making up for a drop-in value even after short-term swings in the market isn't always easy.

For example, if a stock drops by 50% of its value it will actually need to rise by 100% just to get back to even again. Let's say the value of a stock starts out at $10 per share and it drops by 50%. The value of the stock is now $5. If the value then rises by 50%, it will only be worth $7.50. Therefore, in order to get back to its original value of $10 per share the stock would actually need to gain 100% , which is twice as much as it originally dropped.

While you cannot avoid market risk, a well-diversified investment portfolio which includes bond funds, ETFs and municipal bonds may help counter some of the risks of investing in too heavily in individual stocks or equity funds.

Inflation Risk

Inflation is another key risk and over time can affect not only the value of your investments but the generation of retirement income as well. One reason for this is because people are living much longer today and need their income to last for a much longer period.

Inflation risk is defined as "the chance that the cash flows from an investment won't be worth as much in the future because of changes in purchasing power due to inflation."[1] Inflation, in economic terms, is the increase in the cost of living as the costs of goods and services increase.

Think about how much the prices of our basic necessities like gas, food, and utilities have risen over just the past ten years. All of these are necessary purchases, whether you are retired or not. Not only is a long-term stream of income necessary but so is ensuring, as much as possible, that this long-term stream of income will continue to rise over time to keep up with increasing prices.

For example, if the average inflation rate is just over 3%, it can essentially cut your purchasing power by one half in just a 20 years. This means if you retired today, your income would have to double in 20 years just to purchase the same goods and services that you purchase now. So, if your investments are generating $4,000 in earnings per month now, those investments will have to generate $8,000 in earnings per month 20 years down the road just to keep pace with inflation.

How Does Inflation Impact Retirement Income Needs?

Age	25	45	55	65
Income*	$41,951	$51,272	$51,714	$48,685
Anticipated Inflation Rate**	3%	3%	3%	3%
Retirement Age	65	65	65	65
Life Expectancy Age	85	85	85	85
Percentage Of Income To Replace At Retirement	75%	75%	75%	75%
Income Needs Today	$31,463	$39,107	$38,786	$36,514
Annual Income Needs Would Increase To	$102,634	$70,632	$52,124	$36,514
At Age 85 Annual Income Needs Would Be***	$185,369	$127,569	$94,143	$65,948

*Average American Income Salary By Age – smartasset.com
**U.S. Department of Labor
***To maintain the same standard of living today

Interest Rate Risk

Interest rate risk is the risk that the value of an investment will decrease as interest rates rise. 'Interest" is the cost of borrowing money and interest rate is the percentage of the amount of money borrowed.

Interest rate risk can be especially worrisome to those who portfolios are heavily invested in bonds as the value of the bonds may rise or fall based on an interest rate change.

As an example, a bond paying 5% will be worth more if interest rates fall. This is because the holder of the bond is receiving a fixed rate of interest in relation to the market, which is offering a lower rate of return as a result of the decrease in interest rates. If interest rates rise the bond will be worth less because it pays less than prevailing market rates.

Here again, one of the best ways of reducing this type of risk is to have a well-diversified portfolio. For someone who is already retired this could mean investing in fixed income vehicles (e.g., bonds, CD, ETFs) which offer different timeframes paying out a return on a fixed schedule.

Changes in interest rates can be risky in other ways too. They can impact the cost of borrowing money, as well as one's ability to obtain, or not obtain credit. When interest rates rise, it can make borrowing money much more expensive which means that getting a mortgage, a car loan or any other type of loan much more costly to pay back. When interest rates become too high, they can even prevent some borrowers, primarily those with lower credit scores, from being able to obtain loans at all.

Interest rate risk can also affect the value of stocks. When interest rates rise a company's ability to borrow money also rises. Borrowing can be a sign a company is struggling and if so, its stock may be negatively impacted.

Sequence Risk

Sequence risk is a danger that not many investors are aware of. Sequence risk can occur when the return on an investment plunges at the wrong time, such as when you are taking withdrawals but not investing more money to offset the withdrawals and/or losses.

Investors are often told that short-term market fluctuations don't really matter as long as the overall return is positive. Once you retire, even during the few years leading up to retirement, a "down" year in your portfolio can have a long-term negative effect on future income and the value of assets going forward, ultimately depleting money much faster.

As a retiree you are not likely investing more money in your portfolio. When the markets are positive and investments are earning gains, withdrawals can be offset by the gains. If, however, the markets are performing poorly, withdrawals can negatively impact the value of your portfolio as there will be no gains to offset the withdrawals.

For example, Investors A and B each start out with $100,000 in their portfolios and each uses a withdrawal rate of 9%. Both portfolios have an overall return 7%. Investor A's portfolio experiences a negative overall rate of return in year two as opposed to in year three. Investor A's portfolio runs out of money six years earlier than Investor B's portfolio

Investor	Year 1	Year 2	Year 3	Ave. Return	Years Until Depleted
A	+7%	-13%	+27%	+7%	18
B	+7%	+27%	-13%	+7%	24

Source: Government Accountability Office, June 2011 *Interest Rate*

Even if we can agree that the market over time averages 7% return a year it doesn't mean its 7% every year. In other words, it could be negative 15% one year, and then plus 9% the following year, etc.

It is essential that once you begin taking withdrawals from your portfolio you are mindful of not only the gains or returns but how withdrawals impact your portfolio. In a down market taking withdrawals can impact the growth of your assets when the market does recover and turns upward. Can you afford to reduce the amount of withdrawals during a down market?

Longevity Risk

Today, people are living longer life spans than ever before. Even though this is great news, it makes maintaining lifetime income more difficult as you need to stretch out your savings for a much longer periods, maybe even up to 20 or 30 years, and sometimes even longer. Retirees used to be able to live on the income that they received from pensions and Social Security. Income from personal investments was typically just a supplemental or a secondary source. Today, with the disappearance of defined benefit pension plans, coupled with the uncertainty of Social Security, retirees are relying more and more on income from personal savings.

The issue is compounded by other risks that include, inflation, order of returns, and market risk. Not only are you subject to financial risks, but longer life spans mean you are subject to all of these risks for a longer period of time. In addition to that, longer life spans will also mean that many of us are subject to an additional financial risk such as, the need for health care and long term care.

Mitigating Risk

In retirement you want to avoid risk. One of the best ways to remain active across a broad spectrum of assets, while at the same time helping you to reduce risk, is by diversifying your investments. Investopedia defines diversification as being "a risk management technique that mixes a wide variety of investments within a portfolio."

The rationale behind diversification contends that a portfolio that has different types of investments will, on average, yield higher returns as well as pose a lower amount of risk than any of the individual investments that are within the portfolio. So, spreading your investments across a wide range of options can be a good way for you to reduce your risk along your journey, while also allowing you to drive faster than just the minimum speed limit.

Diversity is key to portfolio planning. Risks of the market cannot be avoided so it is important to plan properly by reducing volatility, monitoring expenses and investing in products that produce income. Mitigating risk can only be achieved by regular reviews of investments and investment objectives.

Just as you should have a diverse portfolio you should have diversity in your lifestyle to ensure longevity risk is mitigated. This includes living a healthy lifestyle by eating well, exercising (both mind and body), scheduling physical exams on a regular basis, maintaining positive relationships, and nourishing your contemplative self.

Recognize Market Risks ☐
Do you understand types of risks?
Do you know your risk tolerance level?
Is your portfolio diverse?
Do you rebalance your portfolio?
Other?

Sources

1. https://investinganswers.com/dictionary/i/inflation-risk

Chapter 8: Deal With Debt

Debt is that which is owed; usually referring to assets owed but the term can also cover moral obligations and other interactions not requiring money. A debt is created when a creditor agrees to lend a sum of assets to a debtor. In modern society, debt is usually granted with expected repayment including, in most cases, interest.

Increasingly, retirees and near retirees are faced with debt at levels not previously seen. Credit card debt, mortgage debt and tuition debt are among the top reasons for debt. Illness, early retirement, whether or not by choice, and poor planning based on unrealistic expectations also contribute to the problem. Carefully managing your debts is one of the keys to a secure retirement. We need to determine what type of debt yours is and how you can eliminate it.

Credit Card Debt

In some business situations debt is actually a way toward creating growth. Over the past couple of years, we have seen how banks have used derivatives and loans on risky ventures to bring economies to the brink of disaster. Bank bailouts, such as with Greece, where projected defaults on loans led to billions being loaned to avoid its being destroyed by the debt, prove that even savvy finance leaders don't always have the understanding on how too much debt can affect even a huge institution or a country.

The inverse is true, however, when it comes to personal debt or consumer debt. Individual debtors don't have the luxury of the International Monetary Fund to bail them out of debt.

Consumer debt is that which is used to fund consumption rather than investment and remains unpaid. For instance, consumer debt can be represented by goods or services purchased using a credit card and that credit card has not been fully paid off since the original purchase. This is not 'good debt' as interest rates are high and there is not a tax write off.

If you are holding on to high-interest credit card debt or other similar obligations, it is essential that you rid yourself of these as soon as possible. Credit card companies charge interest rates that can exceed 20%, and if you don't pay off your balance each month, this can add up quickly.

By eliminating this debt, you not only rid yourself of an additional monthly payment, but the money used to pay off the debt can then be shifted to savings and investing, with the added plus of improving your credit score.

Mortgage Debt

Mortgage debt is created when money is borrowed to purchase real estate property with the property itself as the collateral for the borrowed money. Failure to repay mortgage debt, which includes the amount of the loan plus interest, will result in forfeiture of or giving up the property.

Homeownership is very much a part of American life and with it comes financial commitment. As we approach or consider approaching retirement it is important to review the costs associated with living arrangements to determine the best option.

There are many things to consider when deciding whether or not to pay off mortgage debt prior to retirement (assuming a primary or secondary residence):

- What is the current mortgage monthly payment?
- Are you paying mortgage insurance?
- If so, what are the costs?
- What are the costs to improve or maintain the home?
- Is the property where you want to live?
- Do you need all of the space you currently have?
- Will the property be suitable should there be a decline in health?
- Will current assets provide enough income after retirement to continue payments?
- How do school and property taxes impact your budget?
- What assets will provide the income to make payments in retirement?

Paying off a mortgage sooner rather than later will free up income and those mortgage payments can then be transferred to savings and investments, particularly tax deferred investments (e.g., IRA, 401(k)).

Also, with an older loan, payments tend to be applied to reducing principal with the interest tax deduction less applicable. Depending on the interest rate associated with an existing mortgage it may be worthwhile investigating refinancing the mortgage.

If you have a lot of credit card debt, it may be more prudent to payoff high interest credit card debt before paying down a mortgage.

Tuition Debt

Tuition debt is not limited to the younger generation. According to the Consumer Financial Protection Bureau (CFPB), Americans 60 years and older owe more than $86 billion in unpaid college loans. Forty percent of them 65 and older are in default.

Many are in default on their own loans, having taken loans to advance their careers and earning potential with additional education and degrees. Others are in default for loans taken out in an effort to help their children and grandchildren with higher education costs. In some cases, tuition debt is the combination of both; individuals looking to advance their own careers while also assisting their children obtain a college or graduate degree.

Inability to repay all or part of a student loan may be triggered by career choices that don't provide enough income or unexpected life events such as divorce or illness. It is very difficult to obtain forgiveness on student loans, whether federal or private. Failure to repay Parent PLUS Loans (federal student loan program available to parents of dependent undergraduate students), can even result in the government garnishing payment from social security benefits. And, for those whose income becomes fixed in retirement, the burden is even greater.

There are ways to deal with student debt. For example, there are income-driven repayment plans which cap monthly payments based on a percentage of your discretionary income for up to 25 years. This provides a more affordable payment over a long period of time. Refinancing through a private company may be an option allowing you to implement a plan that fits your current budget allowances.[1]

Some Ways to Reduce Debt

The most important aspect to reducing debt is a willingness to change and a commitment to that change.

Calculate Debt

The first step is to calculate the amount of your debt. Start by preparing a list of sources of income and the amount of income generated each month. Calculate, if possible, both gross and net (after taxes).

Next, create a list of fixed and variable expenses. Fixed expenses include, but are not limited to, mortgage payments, car loan payments, medical insurance payments and insurance payments (homeowners, car, life). Variable expenses include, but are not limited to, groceries and entertainment.

Subtract expenses from assets to calculate outstanding debt.

Create a budget

Creating and sticking to a budget is crucial to reducing debt as is understanding and accepting it will include sacrifice. You need to identify income and expenses and then take a hard look at which expenses can be reduced while also avoiding adding additional debt. The best way to do that is to prioritize expenses and determine which are essential versus non-essential.

Even essential expenses, such as, food, shelter, and utilities can be reduced by economizing and changing daily habits. Take advantage of sales, use grocery store savings cards, and switch to less expensive media plans (e.g., cable, cellular). Non-essential expenses may not need to be just reduced but perhaps eliminated altogether.

And if you share these expenses with others (spouse and children), you will find the process more successful if everyone understands the end goal, which is freedom from debt.

Maximize Payments

Maximize the monthly payment on at least one debt, either the largest balance or highest interest rate, while continuing to make minimum payments on the remaining debt. Eliminating a source of debt through maximized payments will free up income to continue eliminating other debt.

Consolidate Debt

If the debt is not too extensive it may be worth consolidating the debt by transferring to a zero or low interest credit card and making payments in full.

Negotiate With Creditors

Depending on how the amount and age of outstanding debt, the creditor may be willing to negotiate a lower interest rate or accept a lump sum payment that is less than one hundred cents on the dollar.

Refinance Your Mortgage

Some of the advantages to refinancing a mortgage include:

1. Lower monthly payments
2. Lower interest rate
3. A reduced term (i.e., from a 30 year adjustable to a 15 year fixed).

Earn Additional Income

Create income by returning to the workforce, turning a hobby into an income producing stream, and/or selling unnecessary items in your life.

Sell Your Current Home, Purchase A Smaller Unit or Rent

An important part of retirement planning is determining where you want to live and why you want to live there. Are your housing costs keeping you from retiring when you want to? It might make sense to sell your current home and purchase a smaller unit in an area with a lower cost of living thereby freeing up funds to pursue other retirement goals. Renting has advantages as well:

1. Fewer maintenance responsibilities and costs
2. No market risk
3. No direct payment of property taxes

Debt After Death

Debt does not necessarily go away after death. Upon death, paying outstanding debt becomes the responsibility of your estate through the probate process. Your estate is responsible for the debt obligations you created. If you die with a will the executor or administrator is responsible for qualifying all debt and satisfying that debt with assets in your estate before distributing any assets to named heirs. If you die without a will, or intestate, the state where you legally resided will take over the process.

In general, beneficiaries are not responsible for the debt of the deceased. If, however, the debt was co-signed by another (e.g. credit card, loan), you lived in a community state (Alaska, Arizona, California, Idaho, Louisiana, Nevada, New Mexico, Texas, Washington, and Wisconsin), or shared a jointly owned property, spouses and/or joint or co-owner(s) may be responsible for satisfying the debt. Authorized users of credit cards can be held responsible for debt incurred after the primary account owner has died.

Certain assets like retirement accounts, insurance policies and annuities which specifically designate beneficiaries and thereby avoid the probate process are generally exempt from having to satisfy the deceased's debt.

Should your estate be insolvent upon your death (the debt is greater than the value of assets), beneficiaries are generally not responsible for the debt. However, a creditor might make a case to hold a beneficiary liable if it can be proven an asset was fraudulently transferred shortly before the owner's death. For example, real estate property transferred shortly before the owner's death after which it was determined the owner was terminally ill with only a few weeks to live.

Professional Advice

It is necessary to consult with a financial advisor and tax preparer when considering how and when to pay off debt. Unless you have significant assets in a non-retirement account, selling some of those assets may require they be replaced in order to have a sufficient source of income in retirement. Planning ahead provides the opportunity to enter retirement with little or no debt. Reducing and/or eliminating debt not only eases the financial burden itself but also the mental and emotional burdens that come with owing debt.

Deal With Debt ☐

Have you determined how much debt you have?
Do you have a strategy to eliminate debt?
Have you considered debt consolidation?
Is the debt in your name only? Or shared?
Will debt impact your estate upon death?
Other?

Sources

1. https://www.forbes.com/sites/robertfarrington/2019/05/22/the-growing-trend-of-retiree-student-loan-debt/#65e0501746a4

Chapter 9: Understand Your Investment Strategy

As you map your retirement, you will encounter detours or side streets you are unfamiliar with. That's why it's important to stay focused on your ultimate destination.

If you construct a building with a strong foundation based on an organized plan of assembly, your building won't just last, it will be sturdy and reliable. Investors who don't know why they are doing what they are doing won't do it for very long. And it definitely won't be done well. The lack of discipline and an absence of proper planning are the biggest causes of failure amongst investors, especially retirees. The best way to get people to stay the course is to make sure you know the why behind your portfolio design.

Build a Balanced Portfolio

One of the best ways to do so is to build a balanced investment portfolio. You may hear stories about "hitting it big" or "striking it rich" with just one or two "hot" stocks but the truth is that real wealth is created by building a solid foundation and growing your funds from there.

In order to build a successful balanced portfolio, you will need to determine certain factors including your investment time horizon, your preferred investment style(s), and your tolerance for risk. A balanced portfolio will include a variety of asset classes with an asset allocation that caters to your investment goals within a changing economic environment.

Know Your Time Horizon

Your investment time horizon is the length of time you have to invest between now and the time you would like to retire. Generally, the shorter the timeframe the less risk you will want to take which can impede having enough for retirement.

Each of the investments that you purchase will also have its own time horizon. When considering a particular investment, it is important to consider how long to hold the investment. How long to hold an investment is influenced by your overall objectives, your growth and/or income needs, as well as your tolerance for risk.

Usually, a short-term hold is less than three years, a mid-term hold is three to ten years and a long-term hold is over ten years.

Short-term hold investments tend to be less risky, like CDs, money market funds or Treasury bills, with the focus on liquidity rather than growth. These types of investments have a lower return rate than longer held investments.

Mid-term hold investments allow for growth and include stocks, mutual funds and ETFs (Exchange Traded Funds).

Long-term hold investments allow for more growth and risk as the timeframe between the purchase and sale may be ten years or longer. Long-term hold investments include stocks, mutual funds, ETFs and bonds.

Investment Styles

Investment style refers to your preferences when it comes to types of investments. Just as we have our own unique personality, investors have personal preferences as to how they go about investing. Some investors dive in headfirst, full steam ahead while others take a more cautious approach. Knowing your investor personality type is important because it will help you in charting your course and staying on course.

Primary investment styles include:

Growth

Growth investors typically have a goal of producing a high return from their invested funds. Many of the investments in this category have a higher price volatility than those that are in the income or growth and income category.

Income

Income investors are more willing to take on some risk and seek investments that will produce cash flow in return for their invested funds. In other words, these investors are seeking "yield".

Growth and Income

Growth and income investors take on somewhat more risk than income-only investors in exchange for obtaining both current income along with the opportunity for their principal to grow faster than the rate of inflation.

Value

The value investor looks for stocks that trade for less than their intrinsic value, seeking out stocks of companies that they feel are undervalued in the market. This provides the opportunity for profit by purchasing stock when the stock price is deflated.

Risk Tolerance

Another important element when building a portfolio is to know what your risk tolerance is and then to invest within those parameters. Investors should have a realistic understanding of their ability to stomach large swings in the value of their investments. Those who take on too much risk and panic when the value of their investments decline can incur unnecessary and costly losses by selling at the wrong time.

You should go into every investment knowing what your true risk tolerance is. If you are not comfortable with a particular investment, then you should forgo it and move on to something else that will allow you to sleep at night.

Asset Classes

Asset class is a group of investments that display similar characteristics and behave similarly in the marketplace. Each asset class offers a different degree of risk and will respond differently to market conditions. A successful portfolio will encompass a variety of asset classes. As conditions or situations change in the market and/or for you it is important to review your portfolio and make sure the asset allocation is working for you.

Some of the asset classes to choose from include:

Stocks

When you invest in stocks, also called equities, you have the opportunity to increase your wealth a great deal.

When you own a share of stock you become a part owner of the company that issued and sold the stock. It is that ownership structure that gives a stock its value. Typically, the value of a stock will correlate to the earnings of that company. The value of a stock may also be based on projections of the company's future earnings.

Throughout the years, stocks have been considered to be very solid investments - for the most part. As our economy has grown, so have corporate earnings as well as the prices of many companies' stocks.

On average stocks have returned approximately 10% over time. The term "over time" can be relative and with the volatility of the stock market the return on individual shares can also be unsettled.

In the short-term, the behavior of the stock market is affected by economic news (e.g. a change in interest rates), environmental conditions (e.g. hurricanes), and investor behavior (e.g. bull versus bear market and supply and demand). Over the long-term it is primarily company earnings and performance that determines whether the price of a stock will go up or down or sideways.

Regardless of what the current market conditions are, investing in stocks should be considered as a long-term endeavor focusing on solid companies with strong track records.

Fixed Income (Bonds)

Bonds can encompass a wide variety of different financial instruments; each with varying degrees of risk and reward. Governments and businesses issue bonds in order to fund their day to day operations or to obtain the funds that are needed for the financing of certain projects.

When you invest in a bond you are lending your funds to the issuer of that bond for a certain period. In return for your loan, you, the bond holder, will receive back the original amount of your investment at a scheduled time in the future along with regular payments of interest.

The price of a bond will increase when interest rates go down and conversely, will decrease when interest rates go up.

If you hold on to a bond until it matures- the date when you can redeem the bond, market fluctuations will not matter as much. You will still receive the original amount that you paid plus your regular payments of interest over time. If you decide to sell the bond before its maturity date you run the risk of trying to sell when interest rates are higher than when you purchased making the bond less attractive to a new buyer.

Many older investors invest in bonds so that they can receive a fixed retirement income from regular interest payments. It is important to also include some growth-related investments such as stocks in the portfolio to help keep pace with inflation, otherwise future purchasing power can be diminished.

Cash

Cash or cash equivalents (e.g. money market accounts) are considered liquid with accessibility to easier and faster than stocks. Having sufficient cash can provide a better sense of security in a down market as well as allow for taking advantage of reduced prices for riskier investments.

Real Estate and Tangible Assets

Investing in real estate, or other tangible assets like gold or natural resources, provides additional diversification in a portfolio. Real estate values tend to fluctuate less than stocks or bonds and can generate revenue through rental income and commission income (e.g. buying and selling).

Other Asset Types

In addition to asset classes, which in and of themselves maybe a type of investment (e.g. stocks, bonds), there are many other types of assets to choose from.

Some of the most common types of investments:

- **Certificates of Deposit (CD)** - Certificates of deposit are time deposits that are typically offered to investors through banks, credit unions, and investment companies. These are considered to be good, safe savings vehicles because they are insured and virtually risk free from market fluctuations. A CD has a specific fixed term and rate of interest. The interest rate on a CD is usually higher than that of a savings account. Common timeframes to hold CDs are 3 months, 6 months, 1 year, and 5 years. It is expected the owner of a CD will hold the investment until the time it matures. At that time, the money may be withdrawn, along with the interest that has been accrued. If, however, the investor cashes out of the CD early they will typically be charged a penalty.

- **Mutual Funds** - A mutual fund is made up of a pool of money that has been collected from numerous investors. The purpose of a mutual fund is to invest in a variety of different securities which may include stocks, bonds, money markets and other types of assets. Mutual funds may pool money from hundreds, or even thousands, of investors in order to construct a portfolio. When an investor purchases shares in a mutual fund they will get a stake in all of its underlying investments. A mutual fund is operated by a money manager or a group of managers whose job it is to invest the fund's capital in line with its stated objectives. Mutual funds are actually purchased in units or shares. These units are issued and can be bought or sold at the fund's net asset value (NAV) per share. A key advantage of investing in mutual funds is that an investor can gain access to a well-diversified portfolio without having to invest a large amount of money. In fact, some mutual funds will allow you to begin investing with as little as $100.

- **Exchange Traded Funds (ETFs)** - An exchange traded fund is a type of security that tracks an index, a commodity, or even a group of assets in a similar manner as an index fund. However, an ETF will actually trade like a stock on a market exchange. These vehicles will also have regular price fluctuations throughout the trading day. Like a mutual fund, ETFs contain a "basket" of many different stocks and other financial assets that are all combined into one single investment. Also similar to a mutual fund, ETFs are sold as shares via the open market to investors. Typically, the goal of an ETF is to match the return of a certain market index (or multiple market indexes).

Investment Costs and Fees

Regardless of the type of financial investment, you can expect to pay a fee, commission or transaction fee. Investment costs need to be considered when factoring in the overall return, because it will make a difference in what you "net" from investments.

Types of investment costs include:

- Management fees which are a percentage of total assets managed.
- Transaction fees which may be assessed for each order to buy or sell a stock or mutual fund.
- Internal expense fees which are associated with the operating expenses of a mutual fund.
- Front end load fees which are deducted from the initial purchase price of an investment like a mutual fund.
- Back end load fees or surrender charges which are assessed when the investment is sold and will vary depending on how long the investment was held.
- Custodial fees which are annual maintenance fees assessed retirement accounts and cover the costs of reporting activity to the IRS.

Asset Allocation

Asset allocation is the strategy used to keep your portfolio balanced. It involves knowing what your financial goals are, what your risk tolerance is and what your investment time horizon is.

The rule of thumb to keeping a portfolio balanced is to deduct your current age from 100. The answer is the percentage of your portfolio that should be invested in stocks. The remaining percentage should be invested in bonds and cash. If you are 40 years old now, 60% of your retirement investment portfolio should be invested in a variety of stocks. The remaining 40% of your portfolio should be in bonds and cash.

Why is this the rule? It goes back to the premise that as we get older, we should take less risk. Because stocks can be volatile it makes sense to re-allocate to bonds and cash which are more stable as we get older.

On the flipside, bonds and cash are victims of inflation. These investments usually do not grow at a rate that keeps up with or is higher than the inflation rate. For example, bonds and cash may grow at a rate of 2% per year while inflation may increase by 4% per year. In this type of a scenario your portfolio is not growing enough to cover inflated costs.

By decreasing the percentage of stock investments in your portfolio you are also decreasing your buying power as inflated costs of goods and services will reduce bond earnings and cash.

Balancing and Re-Balancing

In its simplest terms, balancing your portfolio means keeping a pre-determined percentage of stocks, bonds, cash, and other investment in your retirement account. Re-balancing your portfolio means selling off some of the assets that have gained value and replacing them with some less expensive investments.

Why rebalance?

As an example, your $100,000 portfolio has a predetermined balance of stocks, bonds and cash as follows:

Stocks 50%	$50,000
Bonds 40%	$40,000
Cash 10%	$10,000
Total 100%	$100,000

The market has been performing well and the portfolio mix is now:

Stocks 60%	$72,000
Bonds 35%	$42,000
Cash 5%	$6,000
Total 100%	$120,000

The portfolio value has increased by $20,000. However, you have not really made a profit because you haven't sold any stock--turning it into money. And, the $20,000 gain has changed the original asset allocation plan exposing it to greater financial risk. On the other hand, investing the $20,000 gain in bonds and cash will help to reduce the risk.

It is recommended you review your accounts, preferably with a professional financial advisor on a quarterly basis. The general rule of thumb is that you should re-balance your asset allocation when your assets drift 5% or more away from your original allocation plan. A portfolio that is too heavily weighted in one area can be dangerous because the economy moves in cycles, which means your stock holdings could end up plunging so deeply that moving your portfolio back to its original allotment might take years or might never happen.

While re-balancing is not a guarantee against loss, it will do the following:

- Ensures that you'll be buying low and selling high
- Reduces volatility in your portfolio
- Gives you a sense of consistency
- Offers a process in which emotion and guesswork are eliminated.

The Benefits of Professional Management

A much better way to go about your investing is with the help of a professional financial advisor. This way, you will have someone there to help in guiding you along the entire journey. A professional advisor can help you create the plan that will move you towards achieving your short and long-term financial goals. And, they can also provide you with insight on what to do if and when the road gets bumpy. Let's face it, we know that it undoubtedly will.

Understand Your Investment Strategy   ☐
What is your investment time horizon?
What is your investment style?
What is your risk tolerance?
Do you understand the types of investment assets?
Do you know how much you are paying in investment fees?
Other?

Chapter 10: Leave A Legacy

We all want to be remembered. As we move through life many people start to think about what is truly important; not just from a financial standpoint but from a personal one as well.

Legacies take many forms, though perhaps the most common legacy is a lifetime gift or a bequest of cash.

Monetary Legacy

One of the most common ways to leave a financial legacy to loved ones or an organization is to designate them as beneficiary of an insurance policy, trust or will. Upon death, proceeds from an insurance policy will be paid out as will the distribution of assets from a trust or will.

It's possible to leverage small gifts to generate a much larger, more powerful monetary legacy, in just the same way that contributing small annual contributions to a retirement plan accumulate to become a significant source of retirement income. In the realm of legacy building, while far from being the only way to leave a monetary legacy, the most common vehicle employed is a life insurance policy.

Gift of Life Insurance

With life insurance, small annual premium payments can guarantee much more opportunity to an individual or organization you want to leave a legacy than might otherwise be possible. This provides for expanded opportunity; one that can be guaranteed to someone you want to provide the means to have the best and deepest life experience or guaranteed financial security. Or it may be a guarantee to an organization that promotes the kind of good work in the world you want to see done.

Gift of Retirement Accounts

Likewise, with a retirement account. Once the owner of a tax deferred retirement (e.g. traditional IRA, SEP IRA, 401(k)) account reaches age 70 ½, per IRS rules, they must withdraw a minimum amount of money called an RMD (Required Minimum Distribution). This income is taxable at the owner's ordinary tax rate and failure to do so will result in penalties assessed by the IRS. The amount withdrawn is based on a calculation using the owner's current age, a life expectancy factor determined by the IRS, and the value of the account as of December 31st.

The withdrawal rules also affect a beneficiary (or beneficiaries) of a tax deferred retirement account. In the case of a non-spouse, the assets should be rolled over or transferred to an inherited IRA in the name of the beneficiary. As with the original IRA, the IRS requires RMDs from the inherited IRA with the first withdrawal made by December 31st of the next year after the owner's death.

As an example, Ted inherits a traditional IRA from Uncle Joe who passed away January 1, 2017 at the age of 84. The value of the IRA at year end was $135,000. Using Ted's current age of 44 along with the other factors (Uncle Joe's age and life expectancy factor) the RMD is calculated to be $3,401.

As a result of inheriting an IRA, combined with the IRS rules regarding minimum withdrawals, Ted gets to enjoy a small payout each year. This payout will be realized by Ted every year, assuming he does not need to liquidate some or all of the inherited IRA. Of course, any withdrawal is taxable at Ted's ordinary tax rate.

And just like Ted, this kind of legacy planning can be accomplished without jeopardizing your own long-term financial security.[1]

Gifts

Another way to provide a financial legacy is to gift prior to your death. Generally, the gifts are monetary in nature but can also be non-monetary like a car or stock. The IRS allows an individual to gift up to $15,000 per year to another individual and does not require the filing of a gift tax return. If the gift has value greater than $15,000 then the giver must file a gift tax return. Currently, the IRS allows a giver to gift up to $11.4 million over their lifetime before the gift tax will be assessed, which ranges from 18% to 40%. One reason for gifting during your lifetime is because it provides the opportunity to share in the joy of giving and what the gift means to the recipient. It should be noted that a gift to a qualified charitable organization is considered a donation for which the IRS has different taxation rules.

When bequeathing a donation to a charitable organization bear in mind it can be restricted for a specific use which is of importance to you. For example, if you donate to a medical organization you can specify the donation is restricted to a specific area of research or for the purchase of certain medical equipment.

When deciding to donate to an organization, including your children in the process can be beneficial in several ways and add to your legacy. First, it provides the opportunity to discuss your values on giving. Second, it provides for conversation about causes important to you. Third, it can, and hopefully does, provide the opportunity for your children to consider what causes are important to them and how they can support those causes going forward.

A Non-monetary Legacy

Leaving a legacy is not limited to bequeathing monetary gifts to loved ones or a substantial contribution to a charitable organization. More often, being remembered has much more to do with how you lived your life rather than how much you accumulated. It requires self-reflection about what you value, how you want to be remembered and for what you want to be remembered.

Some thoughtful questions to ask yourself:

- Do you have close relationships with friends and family?
- Have you been a good spouse, partner, parent and friend?
- Do you have an impact on your community?
- Do you share your experiences and skills to enrich others?

Important activities for which you would like to be remembered:

- Spending time with family and friends
- Reaching out to those you've lost contact with
- Mentoring
- Sharing accomplishments and failures to inspire others
- Supporting causes important to you
- Recording your life story on video or in a journal
- Sharing your values

Personal Items

As part of your legacy, take the time to consider personal items you wish to leave to loved ones. Gifts of this nature should reflect a special shared interest or experience. The value of these gifts is in the fond memories evoked and not necessarily the intrinsic value. Something as simple as a worn apron as a thoughtful reminder of the times you and your loved one cooked together. Letters or journals describing meaningful events are another way to leaving your legacy.

How to Ensure That Your Legacy Will Live On

Your purpose in life can also move you towards leaving your desired legacy. For some people, the end goal of paying off your debts and saving money for a secure retirement may be enough. But in order to truly have a successful retirement, it should include ensuring that you have not only taken care of yourself, but that you've also taken care of others. That may encompass your spouse, your children, and other loved ones, as well as other people and/or entities that you care about.

Unfortunately, only 56% of American retirees actually plan to leave an inheritance for their children. One reason for this is because most believe that they won't have any money left to leave after they have made it through retirement.[2]

By following a carefully crafted financial plan that works for you, you can end up leaving a legacy; both of love and financial means. Doing so can not only affect your immediate descendants, but many generations to come.

In order to ensure that this occurs, though, it will be important that you map out not just getting to and through your retirement years, but also chart a course for what will happen afterwards. And, just as with any other type of successful plan of action, what I have found in my nearly 30 years of experience, is that this will entail a course that is specific to you.

Leave A Legacy   ☐
Have you considered who should receive monetary gifts?
Have you considered who should receive non-monetary gifts and what those gifts will be?
How would you like to be remembered?
How would you like to dispose of personal belongings?
Have you written letters or journals describing meaningful events?
Other?

Sources

1. Estate, Business and Retirement Planning Specialist, Les Von Losberg.

2. "What Financial Legacy are You Leaving Behind?" Chris Hogan. (https://www.chrishogan360.com/what-financial-legacy-are-you-leaving-behind/)